Wild Turkey

in Colorado and the
Central Plains

Colorado and Surrounding States

J. Michael Geiger

Order this book online at www.trafford.com
or email orders@trafford.com

Most Trafford titles are also available at major online book retailers.

ISBN: 978-1-4907-5451-2 (sc)
　　　 978-1-4907-5450-5 (e)

Library of Congress Control Number: 2015901436

Our mission is to efficiently provide the world's finest, most comprehensive book publishing service, enabling every author to experience
success. To find out how to publish your book, your way, and have it available worldwide, visit us online at www.trafford.com

Trafford rev. 02/05/2015

www.trafford.com

North America & international
toll-free: 1 888 232 4444 (USA & Canada)
fax: 812 355 4082

PREFACE

This book is designed to provide a region specific guide for the new, as well as the experienced hunter of Wild Turkey in Colorado and the surrounding states. Wild Turkey species have been a recent addition to many new states across the continent. The success of this project is a tribute to the many individual state's wildlife departments, and the efforts of the National Wild Turkey Federation.

Historically, Wild Turkey hunting in Colorado was not widely available. Years ago it was featured only in limited areas in the southeastern part of Colorado near Trinidad. By the 1990's, this had changed when transplanted turkey populations became large enough to furnish a moderate degree of observational and hunting success.

My education in Wild Turkey hunting started in eastern Colorado, primarily along the riparian areas in the South Platte River's corridors, and expanded into central Kansas.

Most of Colorado is semi-arid desert, with the South Platte River and the Arkansas River drainages being the only major waterways in eastern Colorado. These riparian habitats are nearly identical in environmental concerns. These riparian corridors and their tributaries, receive less than 15 inches of annual moisture. The extreme temperatures along these corridors can range from around 115 degrees above zero to nearly 35 degrees below zero, for an extreme temperature range differential of approximately 150 degrees.

The frustration that many hunters in Colorado and the west have experienced in learning how to hunt Wild Turkey, is information based. A great deal of published material exists for hunting these birds in the more dense, and wetter portions of the country. These areas are primarily, along the eastern seaboard, in the south, and in the midwest sections of the country. The new turkey hunter in the west, will find many books in the library regarding hunting Eastern Wild Turkey in other areas of the country.

There are unique differences when hunting Wild Turkey in the mountains and prairies of Colorado and the west. I will address some of those critical differences for the birds, habitat, and hunting tactics in this book.

I have included a portion on engineering development of habitat for the small landowner, lease holder, or club, with the addition of a predator control section. I hope to increase the available information on habitat development for riparian corridors in semi-arid climates. My goal is to provide information to assist with small area critical habitat development, focusing on food plots, shelter areas, and other habitat concerns. I have addressed these concerns, with the background of my having many years of personal experience, successful outcomes, and learning failures.

The biggest difference for hunting Wild Turkey in the west, compared to other areas, is to recognize the realities of our limited water, and correspondingly, the acute lack of lush, dense cover. Most of the west has an average annual precipitation amount of 15 inches or less. A given constant in Wild Turkey habitat is that they demand plenty of water. The adage concerning where turkey prefer to roost explains it well, "They like to roost where they can hear their droppings splash into the water."

The introduction of Wild Turkey populations into Colorado, is due in part to the efforts of the National Wild Turkey Federation and the Colorado Division of Wildlife, (now Colorado Parks and Wildlife), who have had the foresight to introduce both Merriam's and Rio Grande species into new habitats in Colorado.

The introduction of Wild Turkey into the plains riparian corridors, has been a learning experience for everyone. Western riparian corridors do provide occasional patches of dense, ideal cover, with large open areas and meadows surrounded by tall, Prairie Cottonwoods and occasional Mountain Ash for roosting. The Wild Turkey success story in these areas, have proven to be a very thrilling, and exciting chapter in Colorado wildlife management history.

Merriam's Wild Turkey, long known for preferring the higher elevations, up to 10,000 feet, (Oliver and Riley 1990) with the stately Ponderosa Pine environments for food and roosting. Merriam's have habituated well to the lower elevations of the plains. Their success in the flatlands has been helped by modern irrigation practices and the abundance of corn, as well as other cultivated crops grown there. Merriam's Wild Turkey are less numerous, then their Rio Grande counterparts on the plains, possibly because Merriam's, reportedly, do not nest their first year after hatching.

Merriam's have crossed readily with Rio Grande birds. The species delineation method that I find to be the easiest and the most practical to use, is in their tail feather tip coloration. If the tail primary and secondary feather tips are solidly brown or white, they are indicators, respectively, of Rio Grande or Merriam's species.

When there is a color mixture within these feather tips of white, brown and buff coloring, most feel comfortable in considering these as indicators of crosses. There does seem to be some slight, nonuniform, difference in size, as well as coloration, between these species and their crosses. That may be a matter of whether the maternal hen was a Rio Grande or Merriam's or a cross. That particular research will be left up to the wildlife biology graduate students to decipher. I remain an ardent observer, hunter, avocational habitat engineer and conservationist.

This book would not have been possible without the support of my wife, Mary Ann, whose love and support for our "little shack on the river", has made this all possible. She has made my life, and that of many cold hunters, far richer and happier.

I also wish to recognize the membership of the Narrows Mallard Club, Inc., the sportsmen and their families who have leased my acreage along the S. Platte River since inception. These dedicated sportsmen have provided much of the "sweat equity" to make our wildlife habitat management efforts fruitful. Their ongoing efforts will continue to provide habitat for healthy populations of all wildlife, including waterfowl, upland game, Wild Turkey and two species of deer. I could not have accomplished this wildlife success story without all of their support. My appreciation is boundless.

Nomenclature note: A group of Wild Turkey is known, formally, as a "Rafter". That term is seldom used in normal conversation, I will use "Flock" or "Group" interchangeably with "Rafter".

Contents

CHAPTER 1: The Western Turkey Species

**CAUTION: If you have never hunted Turkey before; Don't start, it is terribly addicting !

TURKEY SPECIES

There are six species of Wild Turkey in the Americas. (*The Wild Turkey: Biology & Management*. Pg 32-45) These are: **Osceola** (Florida), **Eastern** (Midwest to East Coast), **Goulds** (SW New Mexico/Texas and Mexican Mountains), **Ocellated** (Campeche Mexico). In Colorado we have: **Rio Grande** (Riparian dwellers esp. near corn Midwest to West Coast), and **Merriam's** (Some Prairie and open fields, near corn but prefers Western Mountains and their Ponderosa Pines). Differentiation of species by observation may not be accurate, and DNA determination may be the only generally accepted method of determining crosses.

Rio Grande Wild Turkey

(*The Wild Turkey: Biology & Management.pg 340-353)*

Let's discuss the premier big bird in the west, the Rio Grande Wild Turkey. Their body color has a copper sheen over predominantly brown body feathers, with a lack of white in the secondary tail feathers. The primary feather's tips are brown to buff .

When we mention the tail feathers, we are discussing primary feather fan tips, and secondary feather tips at the rump, and generally accepted for Rio Grande Wild Turkey, are the presence of darker brown to buff tips. There is a noticeable lack of white, they should be brown or buff on the tips.

Rio Grandes are the largest of the two western species of Wild Turkey. In the less well developed croplands of eastern Colorado and the west, mature Rio Grande Toms will range close to 18-20 lbs for average weight, and have been known to reach 24 lbs. Wild Turkey are reliably aged by spur length. Starting in the first year, the spurs grow at a rate of approximately ¼ inch per year until about year 5 when wear becomes an issue. When the sharp point on the spur becomes rounded, the reliability of this method decreases.

Rio Grande turkey, prefer riparian corridor areas. Water and woody plants are crucial habitat where broad leaf plants provide bugs to feed on. Corn fields are also central to their favored habitat because of the high protein content and rapid uptake by their systems. However, pinto beans and on occasion, soy beans, along with milo and millet are acceptable substitutes. Corn remains king on the menu of preferences.

Another important habitat element, is a decent roost. Rio Grande turkeys prefer to roost close to water. Turkey hunting lore explains it this way, "Turkey like to roost where they can hear their droppings splash into the water." Tall Prairie Cottonwood thickets and occasional Mountain Ash stands provide the favorable roost structures in the western states riparian corridors that Wild Turkey depend upon.

Rio Grande
Picture – Michael Geiger

Merriam's Wild Turkey

(*The Wild Turkey: Biology & Management.pg 333-342*)

The second most plentiful species of turkey is Merriam's Wild Turkey. Their body color features a slight copper sheen over purple to blue black body feathers. The most observable trait is the appearance of lots of white on their lower backs and tail feather tips.

Merriam's primary tail feather fan tips are white to very light buff. The secondary feathers in the tail and rump appear to be all white tipped. The predominance of white in these feathers is probably the best indicator of a Merriam's.

Typically, Merriam's seem to be a bit smaller than Rio Grande's of the same age. For comparison, in 2014, on our property in Morgan County, two, five year old birds, of nearly identical spur length, were harvested. The Rio Grande weighed slightly over 21 lb., and the Merriam with nearly perfectly white tail tips, weighed in at 19.5 lb.

Merriam's aging determinates are the same as Rio Grande's. Their spur growth is also approximately ¼ inch per year to year 5 when wear becomes an issue.

The generally accepted theory about the stock to which Merriam's owe their origin, holds a conflict in itself. It seems to be generally accepted that Merriam's are a cross of Goulds and Rio Grande or, Goulds and Eastern birds, depending upon locale. Where crosses of Merriam's and Rio Grandes are claimed, (Colorado, Wyoming, Nebraska, Kansas) the diagnostic imperative will be DNA testing.

Among hunters where both species and probable crosses are prevalent, a good color mixture, in the primary and secondary feather tips, of brown, buff and white is accepted as a Merriam's/Rio Grande cross.

Merriam's
Picture – Michael Geiger

KEY DIFFERENCES BETWEEN MERRIAM'S AND RIO GRANDE WILD TURKEY

A key difference between Rio Grande and Merriam's, (*The Wild Turkey, Expert Advice for Locating and Calling Big Gobblers, pg 25)* is that in general, Merriam's hens do not nest during the spring of their first year, the reasons are still not clear.

To review the similarities and differences between these two species, both do well in riparian environments with nearby meadows, prairie cottonwoods, and with pine, or dense deciduous shelter belts. Merriam's have adapted to a wide range of environments, and have adapted readily to areas and habitat usually preferred by Rio Grande turkey.

Merriam's preferred habitat, not usually sought by Rio Grande birds, is rich in Ponderosa Pines, and scrub oak. Their diet is usually rich in pinon nuts, acorns and juniper berries, as well as red kinnikinnick berries, and wild strawberries. In mountainous terrain, their preference is for areas with heavy snows and fast running streams. Commonly, there are several miles between their wintering grounds and summer ranges.

Merriam's chief dietary characteristic is their ability to vary their diet when needed. For instance in the winter, Merriam's thrive on watercress, acorns, pinon nuts, prickly pear fruit, as well as local grain agriculture products such as milo, and corn.

Rio Grande/Merriam Cross; Note buff /white mixed tippets
Picture – Michael Geiger

TURKEY GENDER DIFFERENCES

(*The Wild Turkey: Biology & Management. Pg 43-44*)

TOMS: Mature Toms, in all species, are the larger gender. Characteristically, they can be larger by as much as twice the weight of a hen of the same age. They can appear to be 3'- 4' tall with their neck extended, when alerted, when they are running to hens, or other occasions, including when they are fleeing.

The Tom's head is usually bright red, but in display it is predominantly blue, white and red, their neck and wattle are brilliant red, and you often can see a snod over their beak in mature Toms. A Tom's chest, head and neck area are key identifying traits. Toms have noticeable beard feathers. Jakes and 2 year old birds have small beards of about five inches or less.   A Tom's head and wattle will be strikingly red at any time of the year, but are most noticeable in the spring. Concerned or worried hens will often show "pink" on their head and neck area. Look for the difference.

In mature Tom's, the display of a full, even fan, will be evident when they are trying to attract hens. The smooth, full curve of the fan will usually denote birds three years old and older. In Jake's, birds of less than three years old, their fans, by contrast, will feature the center 4-6 primary feathers being dramatically taller, rising approximately 3" above the curve of the fan.

Mature Tom cruising
Picture Michael Geiger

Few, after seeing a mature Tom in full courting display, will ever forget it. When a Tom is in display, their body feathers are noticeably puffed, and their body appears round and massive. Their neck and head will be tucked into the body, and the head will appear to be blue and/or white. Their fan is an even 180 degree arched fan. This display is used to aggressively signal territory or hen claim to other Toms.

Tom display
Picture – Michael Geiger

Toms will often appear to stand straight up and be 3'or 4' tall, especially when curious or running to hens. Their necks are bright red and extended when alerted, gobbling, or curious and looking around.

On the roost, when trying to attract hens, Toms have a noticeable, rattling gobble. Sometimes they also will have a deeper sounding voice when using clucks, chirps and putts. Occasionally they will ping, this is a recognition call. This distinctive sound is much like the sonar ping on a submarine.

HENS

Hens are smaller birds than Toms of the same age by about half. The head covering of hens is more heavily feathered. Their head is mainly bluish and white with small amounts of pink apparent. Hens have more feathers on their necks, and occasionally will have a short, poorly formed beard on their chests. Bearded hens are legal to harvest in the spring, and a mature hen may have a beard as long as about five inches.

Bearded Hen
Pictures – Michael Geiger

Usually the tails of hens are most noticeable when they fly. Occasionally, hens will fan display with their tails, much like Toms, except that their fans are much smaller.

Hens do a lot of "talking" and when hens are with poults, a constant stream of "Jenny chatter" can be heard. It consists of clucks, chirps, putts, and lots of contentment chatter to the flock while feeding.

Once the eggs have hatched, and when the poults are two weeks old, they begin to fly, and are able to roost on low branches, out of danger, with the hens.

Young turkey are called Poults. Rafters (flocks) form in the summer and they will contain poults, second nest poults, and mature hens. Poults have a characteristic whistle, usually a single note, repeated several times then a two-note break into chirps.

Hen and poults feeding
Picture – Michael Geiger

JAKES

One and two year old Tom turkeys are referred to as Jakes. They are similar in size, during their first year, to hens, but have a noticeable amount of pale red showing on their heads and neck. The neck will be bare, and there will be a noticeable beard, 2 – 4 inches long. Their tail in display will be an even, circular fan, except for the middle four to six feathers which will rise above the arch of the fan, to square the middle of the fan. Finally the spurs will be round (not pointed) ¼" to ½" stubs.

Harvested Jake
Picture–Mary Ann Geiger

Note the four squared center tail feathers

Two year old Jake, Note the Beard
Picture – Michael Geiger

WILD TURKEY COMMON CHARACTERISTICS

In the spring, the daily habit of Wild Turkeys, is to come off of the roost and feed, keeping lookout for an opportunity to mate. Toms will spend most of the day looking for mating opportunities, while hens, once mated, will be engaged with egg laying, resting and dusting. At early evening, all turkey will feed and water once more before going to roost just after sundown.

Turkeys are extremely wary birds, and live in a continual sense of fight-or-flight when responding to new stimuli. When they choose to escape danger, they prefer to run, rather that fly. Uncanny in their ability to understand their surroundings, one of their chief tools is their eyesight, which is superb. It affords them 270 degrees range of vision. Their second major survival tool is their hearing. Although their external ears are not readily apparent, Wild Turkeys have superb hearing, and are able to pinpoint the location of a sound from as much as several hundred yards away.

Unfortunately for them, as keen as most of their senses are, their olfactory sense, or ability to smell, is poor to non-existent. A typical comment used by turkey hunters to describe a turkey's inventory of senses is, "If turkey could smell, nobody would be able to shoot them."

All species of Wild Turkey seek similar habitat elements and food. They prefer tall trees for roosting. They frequent gullies and sand draws that have runs near heavy cover. Additionally, broadleaf cover, besides protecting young from the visibility of owls, hawks and eagles, will provide insects, and often is found around trees that provide hard mast such as hackberries, acorns, dogwoods, locust seed pods, and berries.

During periods of heavy snow, wild turkey may choose to remain on the roost all day.

LOCATING TURKEY – SCOUTING

Knowing the dietary and habitat requirements of these birds will help you to locate the best areas to scout. About two weeks prior to season, check the area that you plan to hunt for roost trees. These are the largest trees in an area, and are often surrounded with turkey droppings under the branches. The more droppings, the more often the tree is regularly used as a roost. Additionally, look for feathers, dusting spots, trails, and beak marks near water, all should be considered in context of the places that you find them as you scout an area.

Turkey droppings are diagnostic in shape. Rounded, snail, or pig tail shaped droppings are from hens, while "J" shaped droppings are from Toms.

Hen Turkey dropping   **"J" shaped Tom dropping**
Pictures Michael Geiger

Do your scouting quietly, efficiently, and thoroughly. As any unlucky hunter knows, when turkeys are spooked more than twice, they may move at least a mile away, and can take a week or more to return. Their ability to run at 20 miles per hour means that it will take them just 3 minutes to travel a mile. You must realize that your activities when scouting, especially if you try for a broad ranging coverage of an area, are likely to spook birds. They prefer their solitary locations, with plenty of suitable habitat. Use your eyes, ears and brains more than your feet to scout an area.

A premise to begin with is " Who are their neighbors?" Wild Turkey and deer have a high affinity for each other, partly because of habitat similarities, and partly because of the symbiotic alert relationship between the two. Should you find a large number of bobcat, fox and coyote tracks, instead of deer and turkey tracks, you need to look for a more desirable area for large numbers of turkey.

Turkey are highly mobile, their usual home range is about 2.5 square miles in area. Even though you find a roost tree, it is not likely that the same birds will always return to the same tree night after night. A good roost tree may not roost birds some nights at all, due to the birds traveling to a nearby area, that might be just as suitable for roosting.

Look for regular use trails. Birds in an area tend to be habitual in their preference for travel. Gullies, sand washes, with lots of cover nearby, as well as sandy crossing areas, are great places to look. Landing and take-off spots to cross rivers and streams are likely habitual haunts. Heavy cover, roost trees and water courses near corn fields should all be examined.

At sundown, approach roost trees with binoculars to spot birds, and approach no closer than 75 yards. Quietly watch for birds going to roost. You should look to locate your hunting position near designated roost trees. When you do find good roost trees, stay away from these roosts until the season opens.

SEASONALITY

SPRING

During mating season, Wild Turkeys will form large, heterogeneous, flocks in roost trees. When they leave these roosts, Tom's usually will gobble to attract hens for mating. In Wild Turkey talk, when Toms gobble, hens are expected to "Come-A-Running!"

After leaving the roost, Tom's will go directly to live hens, and they will be difficult to call to your decoys or location, until all hens have been serviced by Toms. Toms will gobble more often when hens are scarce. Large, older, dominant competing Toms will chase off younger, smaller Toms and Jakes. These birds will often form into bachelor flocks of small Toms, Jakes, and two year olds. These birds are easily callable. When hens disappear after mating, they go to nest to lay eggs, this is a great opportunity for the hunter to attract the hormone charged Toms.

A Tom's gobbling attitude is their vulnerability during spring hunting. When hens don't respond to gobbles, Tom's will come looking for the source of hen clucks, chirps and putts that you make while calling.

FALL

Hens and poults will form into large, gender specific, highly social flocks for fall and winter. Hens and Poults will respond to high pitched calls and whistles, looking to build larger flocks. Calling is highly effective when using high pitched yelps, chirps, and the high pitched whistle of poults.

Toms form gender specific flocks in the fall and winter, but groupings are smaller. They are somewhat responsive to calling, but, the best response seems to happen if their flock gets broken up. Calling them to regroup after break up, is an effective tactic that works best in heavy cover. This tactic is not recommended when cover is sparse, (ex western states) especially when visibility through cover is greater than 20-30 yards.

Group of Jakes
Picture – Michael Geiger

CHAPTER 2: How to recognize good Wild Turkey country, and hold your Wild Turkey where you want them.

Finding Wild Turkey Populations

Finding Wild Turkeys is substantially harder to accomplish, if there is not adequate, or appropriate, habitat in the area in which you are looking.

Wild Turkey habitat preferences

1. Pine Savannahs – These are open, well treed coniferous canopies, dominated by several different species of pine, especially Ponderosa Pine, with rich abundant ground cover.

2. Oaks and grasslands – Oak trees, (scrub oak included) dominate in the open areas that are mainly grasslands. Large oak trees, that like to dominate open meadows, provide both roosting areas and food.

3. Wooded Pastures

   Wooded pastures are also known, depending on local custom, as clearings, or meadows. They are critical to the sustainability of Wild Turkey populations nationwide. These are identified as being areas of five acres or less, surrounded by treed edges and are the diagnostic identifiers for this kind of area. In riparian corridors, these often are in gallery forests, (forests that form along riparian corridors because surrounding terrain will not support trees), the edges being composed of Russian Olive, Prairie Cottonwood, and Mountain Ash. In mountainous terrain, look for conifers and Mountain Ash, Aspen, and Choke Cherry trees are all appropriate trees to consider.

Pasture at edge of deciduous woods
Picture-Michael Geiger

Riparian Corridor
Picture – Michael Geiger

4. Riparian Corridors
    Streamside habitats provide water sources, critical travel corridors, as well as ribbons of high quality mast producing trees and shrubs. Tall Prairie Cottonwoods usually provide the best roost sites in western riparian areas.

Food Plots and Habitat Development

Developing or enhancing desirable habitat for wild turkey and other upland game species, including quail, pheasant, and deer, is one of the keys to having more turkey available on a small acreage. For most habitat engineers, the most practical plan is to begin habitat development on an area of five (5) acres or less, and utilize one or more of the following recognized methods; natural, mechanical, fire, and\or chemical methods to achieve better habitat.

It is well known that In much of the west, water is scarce, and most often these areas are classified as semi-arid desert, where annual precipitation is 10-20 inches. For development, this limited moisture content calls for structured crop plantings of drought resistant dry land grasses and crops. The best habitat engineers will utilize and maximize established acceptable habitat, such as forested tree lines, gallery forests, or natural and man-made boundary lines where cover is thickest. A big challenge lies in providing acceptable habitat for nesting and poult development, during the first several weeks, until the poults are able to fly well enough to roost out of the way of danger.

An idea for riparian areas, is the fencing off of a small parcel (less than five acres) as "virgin" territory in the flood plain, to incorporate the natural flood processes in the development of this habitat. Designating this area as year-around, "no human involvement" allowed, sequesters and keeps the area pristine. It will provide enhanced understory cover and protection from predators, in the air and on the ground. Fencing also keeps cattle out of the area, and this protects nests. Inclusion of small, two to five acre plots of unharvested Milo, for winter cover and forage, along with providing spring and summer food plot areas helps complete the development.

FIRE

Using fire as a method to eliminate undesirable weeds or plant species, and to enrich the nutrient base of the soil is practical in wetter climates. In the west, extreme care is needed to keep controlled burns contained. The out-of-control, controlled-burns, have been known to burn down homes and outbuildings.

Prior to igniting any controlled burns, you need to examine the plot for the degree of fuel dryness, wind speed and direction. Be sure to have enough professional and manpower help as well as control elements, including notification to the local fire department, and obtain permits when necessary.

Once the subject plot has been burned, all smoldering remnants extinguished, and the ground has cooled, then soil preparation and crop planting can be addressed.

MECHANICAL CONTROLS

Using mechanical means alone is time consuming, and may take several years to accomplish the best plot. Turning the soil can be counter-productive in high wind areas. Throughout the western states, deep earth plowing at the wrong time of year may end in quality top soil blowing elsewhere, and planted seeds not germinating.

No-till practices, inter-seeding, or shallow plowing, along with planting over mulched, undesirable vegetation, is gaining more attention in drought prone areas.

Be sure to leave buffer areas of 10-15 yards wide near tree lines and fence lines. In riparian areas, do the same near water sources. Develop five acre plots, or greater areas, in segments over a couple of years. leaving a middle buffer stand of native vegetation, may increase success.

Winter forage with buffer area
Picture – Michael Geiger

CHEMICAL CONTROLS

Much about the use of chemical controls has been written. As a licensed commercial chemical applicator, educator, and habitat manager for most of my adult life, the rule is that a mixture of different methods usually works best. Incorporating responsible chemical application allows for better control of large problems, where other methods alone fail.

Nobody wishes to ingest or drink unknown chemicals, no matter how dilute. Neither do we want to lose use of our bodily functions, including eyesight, or to sustain organ damage. Certainly, most people also understand that loss of animals is undesirable as well. Responsible chemical application is always appropriate, and the baseline for the use of chemicals is: **READ THE LABEL IN FULL.**

Identifying the proper target weeds is mandatory. Controlling the problems, not eliminating all species is the solution. Your biomass includes grasses, broadleaf plants and wood plants, you need to develop a plan of development.

Before starting, consult with your extension agent, regarding the proper chemicals for the best control of the plot area.

READ THE LABEL COMPLETELY BEFORE STARTING.

Make sure that the product contains the proper **chemical agents** that you desire. Check the label areas of: **Personal Protective Equipment** – *USE THE GEAR SPECIFIED.*

Environmental hazards: Avoid the potential for human, livestock, or crop damage once applied. Wait for the proper safety period to avoid contamination.

Proper label rates: If not certain, ask a knowledgeable expert. Remember that a 1% solution is one gallon in a one hundred gallon tank of water.

If the **target plant** that you want to control is **NOT listed** on the label, you are using the **WRONG PRODUCT** *you will need to go back to the process beginning, and start over.*

IMPORTANT: Once you applicate the proper chemicals to your development plot, **the following is true for all applied systemic herbicide chemicals**, it will take approximately **10 days** for the chemicals to do their work, and circulate through the plants to the roots.

If you mow or turnover the field, before this **10 day** time period has elapsed, or start conducting immediate inter-seeding after application, you will negate your chemical control efforts, and may kill your newly introduced crop.

Using broad spectrum herbicides, (those that will kill all plants) such as those containing glyphosate, (Roundup and Rodeo et al) or using broad leaf herbicides and tank mixes that contain 2-4-D, and other agents, may yield undesirable results in unwanted tree or crop damage.

Remember to always seek professional, or extension agent help regarding application during windy days, future weather forecasts and chemical drying periods, before starting your application. Always use a surfactant with your work chemical, to ensure that the chemical gets to the plant veins. Monitor and stay away from tree root zones, and avoid application directly to water. Your local state agricultural department or extension agent will be able to assist you with your plans.

CROPS TO PLANT

Which crops to plant, and when to plant them, are usually a mystery to the novice habitat engineer. In semi-arid desert environments, using a mixture of drought resistant native grasses, such as side oats grama, sand drop seed, and switch grass, is a good buffer strategy. If your area does not already grow exotic grains, you should avoid them, it will normally take wild game several growing seasons to develop a taste for an unfamiliar food source.

Corn is probably best left to the professional farmer. It's success depends upon a lot of water, proper equipment, intensive labor, and proper cultivation practices for best results.

Millet food plot
Picture Michael Geiger

Dry land grain crop mixes or single variety crops have worked well. A typical mixture contains several different varieties of sorghum milo, sunflowers, millet and maybe prairie clover. Using seed mixtures, and being flexible in your approach, increases your success chances, by allowing you to use one or more of the following strategies:

A - Isolate a small dryland plot for development. The best are located along tree lines and fence lines. A small plot also allows you to prepare and plant the plot with ATV equipment. Small plots reduce labor requirements.

B - Plant milo and millet in mid-June to mid-July, without planning to harvest the crop. In the fall, turn the entire crop back into the soil, which will enrich the soil, and give you a nutrient base to then plant winter wheat in mid to late September as a spring forage crop. You can then repeat the cycle and disc the wheat crop back into the soil in June.

C - For forage and cover plots, plant the winter forage mixture with milo varieties, millet, sunflowers and prairie clover, in mid-June to mid-July. Leave the entire crop standing all year to provide both forage and protective cover for the young of upland game species. Use this as an effective strategy during winter months.

Chufa

A good crop for moist environments is chufa. Normally, it prefers growing in very moist, sandy loam soil, but will grow in some clays and heavy soils. Replanting annually is normally not necessary, discing and fertilizing each spring will be sufficient for several years. Chufa nodules reportedly taste like a cross of almonds and coconuts. Plant Chufa at a rate of 40 to 50 lbs. to the acre and 1 ½" deep, it requires a 90 day growing period. It is a high preference item for Wild Turkey where this crop will grow.

Mixed grain food plot
Picture – Michael Geiger

PREDATOR CONTROL
Is it a feasible solution?

Certainly no discussion about increasing game populations is complete without the suggestion of predator control. The novice habitat engineer usually decides which particular species to target, based on an incomplete understanding of the problem, and anecdotal speculation about which predator to eliminate.

The authority in practical game management, and predator control, is still Aldo Leopold's *Game Management (pages 230-252).* It is still readily available in bookstores or online. His discussion regarding predator control in *Chapter X* begins to explain the difficulty of conducting effective predator control. For example let us take his ideas and look into Northeast Colorado and the South Platte River basin area.

Using a typical diverse inventory of a traditional hunting acreage along the S. Platte River in eastern Colorado, we can try and show the difficulties with single species predator control.

Bobcat
Picture – Michael Geiger

Our Inventory

Turkey nest predators and destroyers: Rattlesnakes, Bull Snakes, Garter Snakes, Green Belly Racers, Milk Snakes, Snapping Turtles, Magpies, Opossum, Raccoon, three species of Skunk, Weasels, Mink, and cattle.

Turkey Poult and Adult Bird Predators: Great Horned Owl, Barn Owl, Screech Owl, Ferruginous Hawk, Red Tail Hawk, Swainson's Hawk, Sharp Shinned Hawk, American Kestrel, feral dogs and cats, Mountain Lion, Bobcat, Fox, Coyote, and Bald Eagle.

Identifying the problem: All of the listed predators, have similar, yet varied diets. Their diets consist primarily, of mice, rabbits, pheasants, quail, rodents, gophers, and often include each other. Wild Turkeys, in all stages of growth, are featured in all of the listed predator diets, but as an opportunity meal, not a staple. None of the listed predators dine exclusively on Wild Turkeys, or any of the other species for that matter.

Raccoon
Picture – Michael Geiger

The Problem: If you target to eliminate just one predator, Raccoons for example, from the matrix of predators on the property, there would then be more Wild Turkeys available for all of the other predators, and the economic rules of food are familiar:

Excessive numbers of animals to feed upon, breeds ruinous numbers of predators.

In essence, to totally eliminate just one predator species, their portion of the target game becomes more plentiful, thus making more food available. Then more predators, of all different species of predators, will show up to take advantage of the increased food source. Environmental balance, for all species of predator and prey in a habitat environment, is the best goal.

Does this mean that we should never practice predator control? No, it does mean, however, that you need to monitor your relative levels of all predators and prey, and when one species gets out of control, and upsets the environmental balance, then you need to exercise measured control to bring things back into balance.

NOTE OF CAUTION: ALL RAPTORS ARE FEDERALLY PROTECTED. NO CONTROL OF RAPTORS CAN BE EXERCISED.

CHAPTER 3: Where and how to find Wild Turkeys

FINDING WILD TURKEYS

Public Areas

The hunting strategy that you employ to find Wild Turkeys starts by determining whether you are going to hunt in public areas, or on privately owned land. Colorado Parks and Wildlife maintains many areas throughout Colorado that are open to public hunting. Check with them regarding Permits needed, (Limited Draw areas, or Disabled Hunter Permits), also procedures for hunting.

Things to check on before starting your hunt on public land: Do you need to sign in first, are sub areas assigned, and do they maintain food plots in the particular area? Is pre-season scouting permitted, and if so, what are the requirements? In Colorado and elsewhere, ATV use may not be allowed in some public, or designated wildlife areas. In Colorado, on CPW State Wildlife Areas (SWA), and on many public access properties, there may be restricted, or no ATV usage allowed.

Private Property

If you are fortunate enough to own hunting land, know others who own hunting land, or are part of a hunting group that leases property that is available to hunt Wild Turkey on, your options are increased.

Check with the private landowner and secure written permission to hunt on their land, (required to be in your possession while hunting in Colorado). Prior to applying for your Limited Draw License, or obtaining an over the counter license, ensure that you can still hunt on their property, should you be successful and obtain the necessary licenses.

Check with the landowner to see if you can hunt exclusively. If not, find out how many others may be using the property to hunt Wild Turkey. This includes neighbors and family that might be hunting while you are there. Information makes for a safe hunt. Check to make sure that you may use your ATV on their property, and the manner in which they would they like you to operate it on their land to ensure respect for fields and crops.

Communication and cooperation are the key elements to maintaining excellent landowner and hunter relations.

Once you have determined the dynamics of the land that you will be hunting, determine your best opportunity areas for scouting prior to season opening date. Your next step is to actually scout the property.

SCOUTING THE AREA

Identifying good potential habitat is critical. You should look for a clean source of fresh water with good to excellent ground cover of grasses, and broadleaf plants interspersed with gravel beds that have nearby roost trees. In western riparian bottom lands, the best choice is large cottonwood trees located in, or around, wildlife open meadows.

Look under large Prairie Cottonwoods for an abundance of droppings, and don't forget to check for well traveled turkey trails. Their presence will indicate that you have located a regular roost location, or consistently traveled pathway. In areas that have large Ponderosa Pines or other large conifers, look for concentrations of droppings on the ground under heavy branches, or on the needles.

Having a corn or milo field located within a quarter mile distance from the above hot spots, makes your habitat selection excellent, as birds will frequent these fields about two times a day to feed.

Watching for concentrations of Tom tracks on "Turkey Highway" trails, to and from their food source, will also help you find an ideal location to intercept them on their food runs.

SIGN

Tom tracks are distinctive in that Toms tend to travel in a different manner than a group of hens, or hens and poults. Toms are more solitary and often alone. Single Tom's tracks often intersect and cross trails of other turkey, and are large, often more than 4 inches from toe to the end of the heel. There is a fourth "toe" or heel that is obvious in their tracks, this heel is in line with the long central toe.

Hen tracks are smaller, and usually show only three toes branching from a center. On mature hens, there is often a dimple, or spot in the sand, not a long toe, directly behind the footprint central point.

Turkey Tracks **Tom Tracks – toe to heel > 4"**
Picture- Michael Geiger

Hen Tracks
Picture-Michael Geiger

WHEN YOU FIND AN AREA TO HUNT

Prior to season open, while you are scouting, locate your preferred intercept point based on land features and topography. At this time, one to two weeks prior to season open, you should decide whether you will erect a tent, build yourself a blind out of loose brush and camouflage cloth, or decide if you will choose to conceal yourself deep into the natural brush cover.

In Colorado and all immediate surrounding states, they caution and urge you not to stalk Wild Turkeys to have better success in your hunting, and for other hunter's safety.

DANGER: Your rambling through the brush, seeking to encounter and shoot Wild Turkeys, will certainly increase your chances of shooting another camouflaged hunter, whose presence to you may be unknown, until you grab that quick shot at a fleeing bird.

It is true, that in stalking your quarry, should you spook a turkey more than once, it is common for edgy Toms to move as much as a mile away. They often will not return to where they have been freightened from for over a week. Be respectful of the quarry, and courteous to other hunter's chances.

Plan your concealed location so that your shot will be around 20-30 yards for shotgun, or closer than 20 yards for bow and arrow.

Pace off 20 yards from your place of concealment, mark it with a stick in the ground, so that you don't have to re-pace it off on opening morning to place your decoys there. Placing your decoys this way, you will know when the bird is in range, based on this marked reference distance.

Make sure that you have an unobstructed 180 degree clear shooting window.

STRATEGY FOR FINDING A TURKEY

Arrive at your shooting position about an hour or so before shooting time. Walk to your blind position as quietly as possible. The location from which you wish to hunt should fully conceal you. Make sure that once you are in position, your silhouette is broken or well obscured. Camouflage clothing is highly recommended because the turkey's color differentiation and perfect depth perception gives them an exceptional advantage.

The use of hunter orange should be avoided because other hunters will see these colors readily, and could mistake you for a turkey in the brush. Camouflage clothing will hide you in your location, but will not hide motion. Remember the very important 3– S's of Wild Turkey hunting; <u>S</u>it-<u>S</u>till-<u>S</u>ilently !

CHAPTER 4: HUNTING TECHNIQUES - Lets go Hunting !

Decoys

Where and how to set your decoys? There is no single answer on whether or when, to use decoys. There is also, no ideal decoy setup. You need to have more than one decoy, just to add variation.

An effective idea is to go test bird responses with your decoy set-ups, a couple of weeks before season. Set up your decoys in different arrangements to see if they attract attention. Try many combinations, single hen, a hen and a Jake, a hen and two Jakes, a Tom mounting a hen. Determine the most effective decoy scenarios. Offering different looks, several times a day, may save your hunt. You may never see the Tom who visits your decoys the first time. Give him a different look the second time. Variety rules.

The location of your decoy arrangement, regardless of which combination is your choice, is very important. Pick a location that provides the best visibility for 30-40 yards away in all directions. It should be open, visible, on the highest point, and a natural look for your location. Pick the top of a slight hill, the edge of a vegetation change area, the middle of a pasture. Whichever you choose, place the decoy a measured, (paced) distance of about 20 yards from your location. With your decoys at a known distance marker, you also know where the 10, 20, or 30 yards marks would be located from your position, and whether or not that bird may be out of range.

Two Jake decoys worrying a hen decoy
Picture – Michael Geiger

Small fall flock decoy set
Picture – Michael Geiger

Be an ethical hunter: Most states, as well as the NWTF, discourage shots over 40 yards because the chances of wounding the bird, without harvesting it, are much greater beyond that distance.

Still hunting: Is probably the safest and the most effective tactic for hunting Wild Turkeys, especially when accompanied by calling and using decoys. Prolonged waits, with infrequent calling, are often the prescription. Sitting very still and listening is far more important than calling often. Using permanent blinds, building heavy brush blinds, or using hunting tents, all work well for those who have a tough time sitting very still. Remember, that just about any sudden movement will be seen by your quarry.

Sit-Still-Silently: remember that camouflage does not hide movement.

Stalking: Stalking wily Toms, discouraged in the western states, works best with heavy or dense cover. You also need to remember that their hearing is unexcelled. Trying to stalk turkey, when leaves, weeds and other vegetation are dry, is not a good idea. Calling while on the move entails moving, stopping and listening, calling, then listening some more. If no Tom answers back, then change your location by 75 yards or so, and try all over again. It is extremely difficult to be successful using this tactic with sparse cover. The highest risk is in being seen while moving. ***PATIENCE-PATIENCE-PATIENCE !!***

Run-and-gun: This tactic also counts on dense or heavy cover to work effectively. Most of the heavy vegetation areas are located east of the Mississippi River. "Run-and-gun" tactics, as well as busting up Tom flocks, are most often mentioned when discussing tactics used for fall hunting. "Run-and-gun" tactics are also effective for highly mobile flocks in dense cover, and sometimes works best if you call while moving.

CALLS

Practice: How often should you practice your calling? The best answer is to practice using your calls all year long, and to practice and learn how to use new calls in the off season before going into the field.

CALLING COMMUNICATION

How often should you call?

How often one should call while hunting, will always be a hotly debated topic. The proper answer is that "it depends". It depends on weather conditions, hunting technique used, and most importantly, the responsiveness of the birds to your demonstrated call skills.

General rule: <u>Calling less often, and as quietly as possible, is usually the most effective.</u>

Calling: Once shooting time has arrived, sit quietly for some time, listening for the conversations of hens (Jenny chatter) and the advertisement of Toms. Listen for the direction that the sounds are coming from, and how far away they are. Wild Turkey can pinpoint calls in a quiet area, from as much as a quarter mile away. Be cautious with that first yelp.

The best general rule is to listen before calling. Remember that turkey yelp as they descend from their perch. Hens cluck as they gather, and Jakes start to "yaup, yaup, yaup, yaup, kee, kee, yaup yaup" as they test their changing voices. Does that gobbler's throaty, reverberating gobble, in response to your call, spike your adrenaline? If so, you are learning to talk turkey!

Before you Call

Once you are on location at your hunting position, sit quietly for some time and listen before calling. Listen for active turkey chatter, as the rest of the flock gathers together. Certainly listening for the resounding gobble of a Tom or two, trying to gather hens, is the best sound that you could hear. Even if you have a locator call, spend time listening before trying to shock a Tom into betraying his presence with a gobble. Just as in passing a football, there are three possible outcomes when using a locator call, and two of those outcomes are not desired. You might shock a Tom into gobbling and reveal his location, or he may become concerned by all of the hoots, and just quietly leave, or, you may hear nothing at all, which will tell you nothing for sure.

Your goal is to encourage Tom's to gobble, and for them to keep searching for hens. Use occasional yelp calling, with puts and purrs to garner and build the Tom's interest after your initial contact gobble.

The objective of calling is to see if you can get the Tom frustrated enough about the hen (you), who won't come to his gobble, that he seeks her out.

For you to help encourage him in his search, several different kinds of calls may be used. Box calls, pot friction and striker calls, diaphragm calls, turkey wing bone yelpers, along with any number of additional, non-traditional, calls can be used. You should know the abilities and limitations of your calls before you make that first scratch in the field.

TYPES OF CALLS
Locator Calls:

Owl Hooter Call
Picture – Michael Geiger

If you are interested in an area that should be regularly traveled or roosted by the birds, a locator call may help you get a better position on that Tom. If you know you are near a "birdy" area, but are unable to hear any Jenny Chatter, or gobbling, then the use of a locator alarm call is appropriate. Using a locator alarm call too often, or more than once or twice in a set location, may silence any possible further responses of the Toms. Be judicious in a locator call's use.

About 15 minutes before shooting time, some hunters like to use an owl or Crow call; the pattern for owls is, " *short, short, short, short, two sec pause, short, short, short, looooong.*" They also may Crow call once or twice to see if they can get a Tom to alarm gobble, which would let the hunters know where the birds are located.

Box Call
Box calls are made from two dissimilar types of wood, the wood sound box is made of one or two chambers. It has a striker top, which is chalked, which is then rubbed against one of the sides. Yelps, chucks, chirps, purrs and putts are all possible, as well as gobbles.

Advantages: Tone and fidelity of box turkey calls are very much like real birds.
Box calls are easy to play, and can easily be used simultaneously with other calls to sound like a group.

Disadvantages: These are Large and bulky, they often squeak in transport, and may not work in wet weather.

Box Call
Picture – Michael Geiger

Pot friction call and striker

Several styles are available. Round plastic molded, or wood formed, "pots" with a variety of tops, such as slate, sandstone, glass and acrylic, are common. The pot does not have to be round, it often will be of a multitude of shapes, and the strikers can be of different materials, sizes and shapes. Strikers are varied, and allow for different external conditions. They can be varied by types of woods, acrylic, carbon fiber, non-skid all weather traction tips and more.

Advantages: High tone fidelity, with a large range of calls and chatter possible. They make excellent yelps, purrs and putts. Their size is convenient, and you can carry more than one easily. They are an excellent choice.

Disadvantages: In wet weather, the top may have to be refreshed often, as will the striker tip. Some wet days you just have the wrong pot top, for the wrong striker or the wrong day.

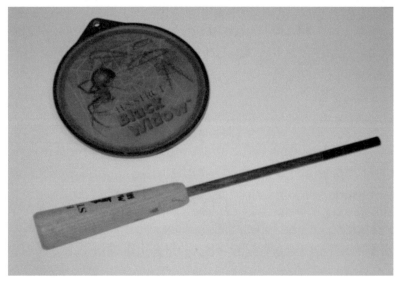

Pot or slate type call
Picture- Michael Geiger

Diaphragm mouth call

This type of call is usually made from vinyl and latex rubber. You put the call against the top-back of your mouth, and blow past your tongue. A wide range of calls are possible. You can make clucks, chirps, purrs, putts, and gobbles, as well as imitate other turkey sounds.

Advantage: This call does not count on movement of arms to work, you can change locations with it in your mouth, it adds diversity and allows different calls and pitches This variability makes it a very good, all- around choice.

Disadvantage: Because it is in your mouth all of the time, over calling, poor calling, and mis-calling are significant risks, as is calling too loudly all of the time. These calls do require a good deal of practice to play consistently.

Diaphragm Calls
Picture – Michael Geiger

To use a diaphragm call, say the following while exhaling through your mouth:

Kee-Kee run: Say "pee pee cholk" Best with high a pitch and to interrupt the air flow with lips.

Clucks and yelps: Incorporate jaw dropping and tongue, say "plock" sharply for clucks, and "cholk" for yelps.

Chirps, Lost bird call: Say "Chiiirp" (draw out 4 times), wait 10-12 seconds then follow with 15-20 yelps.

Putts: Use lips for a sharp "pot pot pot"

Cackling : Tongue and jaw drop work best to say "tist tist, cat cat cat cat, cholk cholk cholk (the use of jaw movement is very important to make calls sound right)

Wing Bone call

These calls are made from the wing bones of turkeys. Synthetic replicas are also available. Wild Turkey bones are preferred, (commercial bird bones are often too large, or too thin, causing them to crack) Two bones of the lower wing (tibia and fibula), as well as upper bone (humerus) go together to form a three piece trumpet type call. More common recently, is just the two bone call, without the trumpet (humerus) end. Wing Bone calls are suction calls that require back suction by the tongue, causing the lip to vibrate against the call, making a yelping sound.

Advantages: Fidelity of tone, and several varieties of pitch changes are possible with practice.

Disadvantages: Individual pieces must be cleaned inside the bone before assembly and use. To play properly, they take a great deal of practice, and they are hard to learn to call softly. Only 3 or 4 different calls can be played, purrs and gobbles are not easily within in their repertoire.

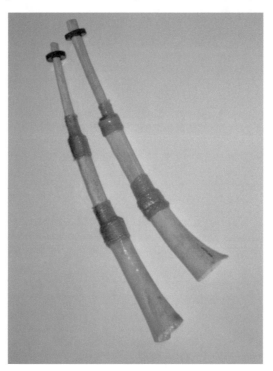

Turkey Wing Bone Call
Picture- Michael Geiger

BEFORE YOU GO INTO THE FIELD WITH YOUR CALLS

Make sure that you can purr a slate, so as not to make it squeak. You should be able to blow a cut, yelp, chirp or putt on your diaphragm call whenever you wish. You also should be able to make yelps on a box call, so that it will ring through the woods. Your wing bone call may sound more believable to the Tom, with your cupped hand over the end.

For the greatest success in your calling, it is imperative that you practice your calling before going into the field, regardless of the type of call that you choose to use.

Other calls

Many different types of turkey call devices have been designed. There are several more varieties beyond these four types. Different materials are constantly being introduced and styles vary widely.

The array of calls, and methods by which these different varieties are played remains the same. The calls will still be of the basic friction type (pots and box calls), exhale or blow (diaphragms), or suction (wing bone). An example would be the push type friction calls and "shaker" style gobble calls available.

The key component for all calls that will help you be the best is: **<u>PRACTICE!</u>** Make sure that your hunting partner welcomes your company because you can call well, demonstrated by a gobbler's resoundingly gobble in response to your efforts.

CHAPTER 5: Harvesting a Wild Turkey – Now that he is here, what do you do?

Whether you are using a shotgun or a bow and arrow, a turkey can be a very difficult bird to kill. With an arrow, the placement of the arrow is critical because you must hit the vital organs, (heart and lungs) . The "boiler room" is about the size of a baseball, and is located just under and behind the wing shoulder joint. What makes the shot difficult is that the critical area is small in size, also because the denseness and texture of the body feathering may act much like a safety vest.

Using a shotgun, the shot placement is also crucial because body shots, most often, do not immediately kill. With a shotgun, you should be aiming at the base of the neck area. Your kill zone is approximately 10 inches long and half of an inch wide. You must place one or more pellets into the head, or spinal column and neck, for an immediate kill.

Shooting a turkey in the body with a shotgun is problematic. First, the feather covering absorbs much of the shock energy and may deflect lighter shot sizes. Secondly, the sheer amount of dense breast meat, eliminates the breast as a realistic target for a shotgun. It has been shown that you need four (4) pellets into the vital organs to kill the bird. _Tom Roster's research on lethality._

TRADITIONAL THANKSGIVING DINNER NEWS-- TURKEY'S WERE HARVESTED IN THE FALL !

Tom Turkey in fall snow
Picture - Jim Butler

FALL HUNTING PRACTICES

Turkey have a brain the size of a walnut, and they do not have the critical connection that gives humans the ability to reason and make logical decisions. Turkey, regardless of what many hunters think, do not have the ability to reason logically. Their eyesight and hearing may be unsurpassed in the wild, but they learn to avoid danger by negative reinforcement. They are on the top rung of most predator's food list, so living in a constant "fight-or-flight" mode keeps them on edge. They do learn to avoid suspicious situations, thus, your calling with the same pattern, too loudly, or too often is seldom a good idea. Turkey communication and chatter is complex, it consists of many sounds and patterns. For the best success, especially in the fall, change up your calling routine, and your decoys.

Fall Decoying

The use of a decoy, or decoy spreads, will often sweeten the pot as an incentive, add confidence, or work as an attractor. Probably the most productive tactic is to locate the flocks source of food, and then set up along their travel route. Fall and winter times require higher nutrient levels to sustain them against the cold and the lack of available feed under the snow. Established routes to corn and grain fields can easily become highways to success.

Avoid placing your decoys in the same spot or same arrangement day after day. You should change up their appearance. In the fall, Wild Turkey gather more strongly than they do in the spring. It is a good idea to use several Jakes or hens to start, then vary the look with odd arrangements of hens, Jakes and Toms, several times a day. Remember, that you may never see a curious visiting turkey. If they do not like what they see and hear, they likely will quietly move on, without you knowing they are in the area. Any Wild Turkey who continually sees and hears the same thing, at the same place, will likely move away to less suspicious territory.

In the late fall, once the leaves have dropped, and visibility is good, using several Tom and Jake decoys to imitate a small flock, may give the impression that a broken flock is regrouping. Once Toms see the decoys, turkey may run directly into the spread. For a single Jake or display Tom decoy, keep it in close proximity to you. In fall hunting, turkey are more vocal than many realize. All turkey sounds are helpful, clucks, lost yelps, assembly yelps, kee-kee runs, cutting and even gobbling should be used.

During both Fall and Spring hunting, listen to learn new sounds of the turkey vocabulary, then do your best to imitate what you hear. Be involved and insert emotion to sell the call. The more eager and urgent you sound, the more frantic and excited the turkeys become.

Other Tactics

To bust a flock, or not, will remain controversial as long as two turkey hunters gather. A critical consideration is whether or not the available amount of vegetation and available cover will let you get close enough to the Tom flock, without them seeing you first.

Busting a flock involves charging directly into a group of Toms, letting them scatter while you sit down and begin calling them back together near your location. For those who would like to bust a flock just as they go to roost; It is a myth that wild turkey will reassemble in pitch dark. Turkey do not see well in the dark.

Roost fall birds the same way that you do in the spring, then in early morning, call softly to get them started, mimicing them as they fly down and gather. To hunt the roost at dawn, set up close, about 75 yards from the roost site. Try to set up on the same side as they flew into the roost on. Be ready with pleading clucks, yelps and kee-kees at first light.

HARVEST METHODS

Whether you plan to hunt and harvest your bird during the spring season, or in the fall, the fundamentals regarding the use of your shotgun or bow and arrow remain the same. Certainly, appropriate dress is always necessary to protect you against the elements. Being cold and wet is never fun, especially when the turkey are quiet and seemingly not in the neighborhood.

Shotgun: The gauge of shotgun that you use is not nearly as critical as the size of shot, the point of aim, and the type of choke that you use. Most all gauges of shotguns have been used successfully. The key is the number of pellets that hit the critical area, at the distance that you shoot. Traditionally, for shot-gunning, 20 to 30 yards is the preferred range. The NWTF encourages shots of less than 40 yards. Shots at Wild Turkey greater than that distance are not felt to be highly ethical, and may result in fewer kills and more crippled birds.

Some hunters prefer shorter barrels, some have a penchant for lots of gun camouflage and long barrels. The shorter barrel is less apt to be tangled in brush at the critical time. Modern ammunition makes barrel length considerations unnecessary for short distances.

What size shot?: Tom Roster is an expert on shotgun shot lethality. His charts are often used as guides. The interpretation of his charts on lethality seem to indicate that for a 20-40 yard distance, you should be using size 4, 5 or 6 shot and that you will need 3-4 pellet hits in the critical area to be able to harvest your bird. Your chances of doing this are best if you use a "Full" or "Extra Full" turkey choke in your shotgun.

SHOT SIZE RESTRICTIONS: Colorado, Nebraska and Kansas prohibit shot size larger than #2 for Wild Turkey. Missouri prohibits using larger than #4 shot. UT, OK maximum size is BB. TX, NM, WY, MT, ND, SD do not have maximum shot size restrictions. *(Check current regulations – above is current for 2014)*

Notice that special attention is brought to a Full or Extra Full choke. When you are shooting toward a Wild Turkey, you must aim your shotgun as if it were a rifle, to make sure that the maximum number of pellets will strike in the critical kill area.

Aim your shotgun/ Pattern your shot

Shotgun wing shooters usually point and shoot at their game. Precise targeting is required in Turkey hunting, and alignment of the barrel, along with proper sight picture of the bead and target are all critical.

Head Down, Cheek on Stock, see the rib and bead, Aim your shotgun and Pattern your shot. Misses occur often due to deflection of pellets.

Aim your shotgun like a rifle.

Aim down the entire length of the full barrel, with your head down, your cheek on stock. If there are two beads, align them to form a figure "8", if there is just one bead, put it on top of where you want to hit.

Caliber, Shot size and Choke

- Caliber is not critical. Most all shotgun gauges will work up to 30 yard shots.
- Shot size and pellet count are critical elements. The larger the shot, the fewer the number of pellets.
- Because of a precise small size target, Full or Extra Full Turkey Chokes are recommended.
- Choke size is very important, especially if you are shooting at more than 30 yards from the turkey.
- Back shots will encounter feathers and bone. If not a direct perpendicular hit, you may not kill the bird, and cause him to be a cripple.

Make sure that your sight picture includes sighting along the entire barrel length, cheek firm on stock, stock butt set right in your shoulder, and use a full or extra full choke. Attention to these details in most turkey hunting will avoid misses caused by pointing and shooting. Point-and-shoot works for wing shooting, not necessarily for turkey.

Learn to aim your shotgun like a rifle

The most effective kill shot on a turkey lies in one of two places, the head and neck area, or the internal organ area. For a shotgun, the head and neck shot is the most effective when the neck is extended, opening up the 10 inch long critical kill area. The easiest way to do this is to wait for the turkey to extend his neck full length, which it will do to investigate something it does not recognize, or to gobble. Shooting at the head when the rest of the neck is tucked, as in when the Tom is in display, is a difficult shot because the critical area is small, and somewhat protected from danger.

The internal organ area is hard to reach with the pellets from a shotgun. The armor-like feathers and dense breast, make front entry nearly impossible; side shots may work from closer range, but wings bones and tough feathers act as armor, and back shots are equally as hard as front breast shots.

Know your tools – Sight in your shotgun

- <u>**Key:**</u> Pellets must break the neck bone, or no fewer than 4 pellets must lodge in, or interrupt internal vital organs

- Vulnerable spots are the neck/ head area, and the side under the wing.

- Breast shots are generally not reliable due to the depth of the muscle and the feather density.

Practical aspects

Sight-in your shotgun with a full or extra full choke tube. Pattern your gun, using the shot size and load of your choice prior to season. Use lead or no-tox, or better yet, pattern both, then pick the one that gives you the best spot-on pattern.

Proper pattern **Improper sight picture,**

Pictures – Michael Geiger

Before you shoot

Check your shotgun for its pattern at 30 yards. In turkey hunting, this should be one of the first things you do before you are ready for the season.

There are many splatter style, and paper practice targets available, that feature the kill zone neck and head of a turkey as a target. Turkey shooting changes the way you must shoot. You need to treat your shotgun as if you were shooting a rifle.

Often, shooting more than once at a bird is a waste of time, and may injure the bird which will likely become bobcat, fox, or coyote feed at a later time. Make the first shot count. Don't waste a splendid resource.

Know your tools – Sight in bow and arrows

Archery

- What distance do you plan for your shot?

- How much kill power is in your shots out to 30 yards?

- Are you using the proper hunting arrow?

WHAT KIND OF BOW?

With a Long Bow, you will notice that it takes more strength to operate. As the bow string is drawn back, the draw force becomes heavier with each inch of draw (and most difficult to hold at full draw). Therefore, little energy is stored in the first half of the draw, and much more energy is stored at the end where the draw weight is heaviest.

Using the Compound Bow, you will discover a totally different draw experience. These bows operate with a different profile, they achieve their peak power within the first few inches of the draw, and then remain flat and constant until the end of the cycle. This concept of maintaining the same draw weight throughout the draw is why compound bows store more energy and shoot faster than an equivalent peak weight recurve bow or longbow. Arrows work best to the organ area. For archery, "greatest mass area" rules your shot.

HOW MUCH BOW TO KILL A TURKEY?

In finding the right bow for you, there is little information addressing Foot Pounds of Kinetic Energy (FPS) delivered at distance needed to penetrate a turkey. Truthfully, it varies depending on whether it is a side entry shot, or a full frontal breast shot. The best information would indicate that, depending upon the size of the bird, a minimum energy range of 18 – 20 FPS would normally be required. it is the job of matching you, the bow and the arrows together to deliver enough kinetic energy to the bird. How do we determine the proper size of bow and arrow to achieve this?

Kinetic Energy = (arrow wt)((bow velocity in FPS)(sq))/2 x acceleration of gravity(KE =(m)(v)(v)/450,240)

IBO Standard rating standard: Draw weight70#, 30" draw length, 350 grain arrow, KE = Initial FPS.

Physics of the Problem: (From IBO information and charts)

Kinetic Energy deteriorates over distance.

On average you can expect to lose an average of 1.5 ft-lbs for every 10 yards of arrow travel. If the arrow has 29 ft-lbs KE at point-blank range, expect this value to be closer to 24.5 ft-lb KE if shooting a target, **located 30 yards** away. This is still enough to take down a well placed shot on a wild turkey.

Draw Length Impact On Speed

For every 1" of reduction in draw length, from 30" standard, you can expect to lose around 10 FPS of arrow speed. IBO speed tests are conducted using 30" draw length, however most people have a draw length of around 26-28". This is already a 20 to 30FPS reduction compared to the IBO speed rating.

Draw Weight Impact On Speed

For every 10 lbs. of reduction in draw weight, expect to lose around 15-20 FPS. For many beginners using a 70 lbs. draw weight compound bow (like the ones used during IBO tests) is not possible. An adult beginner will likely go for a 60 lbs. version. That's another 15-20 FPS reduction.

Arrow Weight Impact On Speed

For every extra 5 grains of arrow weight, expect the speed of your bow to be reduced by about 1.5 FPS. IBO speed tests are conducted using 350 grain arrows, however, depending on the type of game, the weight of the arrow will vary. For example if you use an arrow of 425 grains, that is 75 grains over the IBO arrow weight, which reduces FPS by an estimated 22 FPS.

Extra Accessories On String

Likely you will be using accessories in your bow string. A D-loop and peep hole are fairly standard, which together weigh around 15 grains. This can cost you of another 5-6 FPS.

Release Method Impact On Speed

Most humans are not capable of releasing an arrow as accurately as the machine that they use for IBO standards. So, you'll need to subtract another 2-3 FPS compared to the IBO rating.

There is no standard bow speed among manufactures. The speed of a bow depends on many different factors (draw length, draw weight,and arrow weight are the most important). To arrive at a standard measurement, The IBO developed a set of common testing conditions.

All IBO tests are performed with: A 70 lbs. draw weight version of the bow and A 30" draw length and A 350 grain arrow.

Practical Problem

CAN YOU KILL A WILD TURKEY AT 30 YARDS WITH A 30# BOW, AND DRAW LENGTH OF 26"?

Not everybody can handle a 70# draw weight bow. My body started to fall apart several years ago, and now I have virtually no shoulder, and a rebuilt elbow. A trip to my local bow shop, and a very accomodating technician helped me determine that I can pull back a 25# bow easily, and with development, 30# and maybe 35# might be possible.

- **Real problem:** Weak arm and shoulder

- **Bow**: Mission Craze Bow, IBO rated 306 fps, 30" Draw Length, 70# Draw weight, 350 grain arrow

- **HUNTER PROBLEM:** Distance 30 yds, Draw weight #30, Draw length 26"

SOLUTION CHOICES: Bow: 30 lbs. draw weight version of the bow. Measured personal draw length of 26", and use standard weight 350 grain arrows to start. Your choice is to also install some accessories onto your bow string. **Will these choices work to kill a turkey, if you aim well?**

Practical Solution, here's the adjusted math factors: (Note FPS = foot pounds KE at bow)

BY THE STEPS

- You will lose around 59 FPS due to using a 35 lbs. rather than a 70 lbs. draw weight

- You will lose around 40 FPS due to using a 26" draw length rather than 30"

- You will lose around 0 FPS due to using a IBO standard of 350 grain arrow, which is used in IBO testing (Note: +-1.5 FPS per 5 grains wt diff from 350 grain)

- You will lose around 5 FPS due to extra accessories on the string

- You will lose around 3 FPS due to imperfections in human release mechanics

- Bow Speed is: 59 + 40 + 60 + 5 + 3 =158 FPS that have been lost. This means that the **actual velocity of your bow will be 306 FPS – 158 = 148 FPS.** Now factor in distance and arrow weight:

- Distance 30 yards, You will lose around 1.5 FPS per each 10 yards of distance = 148 – 4.5 = 143.5 FPS KE at target distance.

LETS NOW DO THE MATH:

- With 150 grain arrow: 150(143.5)(143.5)/450,240 = 6.86 FPS KE at target

- With 170 grain arrow: 170(224.5)(224.5)/450,240 = 19.030 FPS KE at tgt (100 gr lighter arrow adds 30

- FPS to formula 30 FPS (-100 gr/5= -20 x -1.5= +30fps 194.5+30= 224.5FPS)

- With 200 grain arrow: 200(164.5)(164.5)/450,240 = 12.020 FPS KE at target (100 gr heavier arrow) subtracts 30 FPS (100 gr/5=20 x -1.5= -30fps 194.5-30= 164.5FPS)

TURKEY SPECIFIC CHART FOR LOW POWER BOWS AND ARROWS

Bow speed 306 FPS @70# & 30" draw

(Arrow wt) ((calc. speed)(sq))/450,240 = FPS KE

Following **figures adjusted for 26" draw, FPS at a 30 yard target,**

10 yd would be (-0.5FPS).

** FPS rounded to nearest half pound

Arrow Weight in grains

Bow Wt.	170	250	300	350
25 lbs	6	12	17.5	27
30 lbs	7	13.5	19	28
35 lbs	7.5	15	21	31
40 lbs	9	18	26	33

Probably too light

Best for side shots only

Probably okay

Good Match Turkey

Chart and calculations created by J. Michael Geiger using reliable information.
This chart has NOT been validated as correct by IBO, or by actual field or scientific tests.

Killing a Wild Turkey with archery

To efficiently kill a wild turkey with a bow and arrow, you will need to place the arrow into the kill area of the body where it will strike vital organs. This is your best target area, and most easily done through the side of the bird, just above and behind the shoulder area. Here again, the toughness of the feathers may deflect or prevent a vital strike, should the arrow strike the body at less than a direct angle. The back offers a target which is mainly feather and bone. Your shot, with the back as a target, needs to be direct, and at a perpendicular angle to the back.

How long to hunt?: Did you plan only an hour or two to bag your bird? Can you stay out all day? Do you only hunt at dawn and dark? Turkey range all day. What kind of pressure do you place on yourself to be successful in a short period of time, when you hunt?

Patience-Patience-Patience !

A well planned, several day long turkey hunting trip makes for far more successful hunts. If you have only Saturday morning to hunt, it may not be as successful as you would like. Sometimes, for whatever reason, Wild Turkey will not respond to your calls, nor come to your decoys. You should always plan your hunt for more than one day in the field. Doing so, ensures a far more enjoyable and successful hunt.

CHAPTER 6: CLOTHING, WHAT TO WEAR

Turkey Hunting 101, Turkey School/Chapter 1. About Turkey Hunting, Page 3. (Paraphrased from Recommendation from Colorado Parks and Wildlife) By Jim Bulger, Hunter Outreach Program Coordinator, 2013

1. Avoid wearing clothing that has the same colors as a turkey. Red, white, and blue are the colors found in wild birds.

2. Protect your back. Find a tree or rock outcropping to back up against and protect your backside.

3. Place decoys in a location that you can see the gobbler approaching.

4. When traveling to a hunting location, transporting decoys or a harvested bird, wear hunter orange (a vest or hat). Place the harvested bird in a game bag or wrap the bird in an orange vest. **DO NOT** sling a harvested bird over your shoulder and walk out of you hunting area.

5. Clearly identify your target as a legal bird before shooting.

6. Never stalk a wild turkey. The enjoyment of the spring season is calling the bird to you.

Dress Apparel and Blinds

Dress head-to-toe in camouflage, utilize face paint or a face cover for your head. **<u>DO NOT USE HUNTER ORANGE</u>** as part of your outfit. When transporting a harvested bird or decoys in the field, wear a hunter orange vest or hat.

ULTRA VIOLET NEUTRLIZATION

How to See and _Not_ be Seen: Wild Turkey have phenomenal eyesight. Besides having a field of vision of about 270 degrees, their eyes have trichromate vision. This means that they see colors exactly as we do. Deer and other animals, have monochromate vision, and see everything as one shade of color hue, often blue or pale yellow. Turkey, besides being able to see color the same way that we do, also see the ultra-violet portion of the spectrum.

The problem for turkey hunters is that turkey can, and do, see materials and colors that are fluorescent, e.g. what we see when things glow under an ultra-violet or black light. Clothing that contains color brighteners, which are phosphate in origin, causes the fluorescence.

Turkey see normal colors, PLUS they see things that contain high amounts of phosphates. If you do not use a neutralizer on fresh washed, or purchased clothes, your camo will have a fluorescent blue glow about you, and the turkey will more easily see your movements.

Many military and tactical response teams are very much aware of this property in their clothing. They avoid UV brighteners by wearing wool, or washing their clothes in "safe" products. There also are products available with which you can treat your clothes, to avoid glowing in the brush.

How to avoid glowing in the brush

Besides neutralizing your turkey hunting garments, and hat, an easy solution is to wear WOOL GARMENTS – the lanolin in wool does not pick up color enhancers.

You can also wash your newly purchased or dirty turkey hunting clothes in products that do not contain UV brighteners. An incomplete, and partial list of some of these products shows familiar names:

- Bold Powder
- Cheer Liquid (all versions)
- Cheer Powder(all versions)
- All Powder
- Surf Powder
- Woolite
- 20 Mule-Team Borax
- Baking Soda

Reducing your exposure with some sort of cover is of critical importance. Once you decide on your hunting location of choice, make sure that your shoulders, and silhouette, are well obscured by the background, or are below the edge of the blind.

Sitting in **heavy cover**; use of **established blinds**; and the use of **game blind tents** are all accepted hunting tactics.

Camouflage-clad hunter in brush cover
Picture – Michael Geiger

Permanent Blind
Picture – Michael Geiger

SUMMARY

SUMMARY: Turkey hunting in Colorado, and in most western states, is a relatively new sport. Most people in this area have not had the exciting experience of hearing a Tom answer a call, listen to hens cluck to their young, or watch Jakes try to steal hens from Toms. Turkey hunting is different from deer and elk hunting, also it is different from pheasant, and duck hunting. However, it does use skills from all of these segments of game hunting as critical components. You need to be able to call well, aim your shotgun like a rifle, still hunt (3-S's), and scout the territory well. In Wild Turkey hunting, knowing what <u>not</u> to do is often as important, as knowing what to do.

DO:

1. Practice calling all year long.
2. Scout your area several weeks prior to season
3. Choose the proper size shot, sight in your shotgun, practice your arrow release before you get in the blind
4. Give your calling many, lengthy breaks, **and LISTEN MORE !**
5. **Be Patient, Be Patient, Be Patient,** and practice **the 3-"S"'s (Sit-Still-Silently !)**
6. Enjoy your hunt, and take a kid hunting soon!

AVOID:

1. **Wandering around looking for opportunities, or trying to stalk turkey. Famous last words "There is a turkey, let's go get 'em".**
2. **Calling continuously**
3. **Noise-loud idle chatter, trips to "fix" the decoys.**
4. **Smoking is always controversial because turkey do not smell. However, they can, and will spot the smoke faster than you can put out your smoke; pipe, cigar or cigarette.**
5. **Unnecessary radio chatter – it can be worse than loud voices in the background.**
6. **Excessive ATV use: Running ATV's for bathroom breaks and coffee.**

PRACTICE SAFE DEFENSIVE TECHNIQUES

Recommendations from NWTF (National Wild Turkey Federation)

1. Never stalk a turkey.
2. Eliminate the colors of Red, Blue and White from your gear.
3. Never make turkey sounds to alert or call other hunters
4. Never make gobbler sounds near another hunter
5. Never approach closer than 75 yards to a roosting turkey
6. **Total elimination of motion**, not total concealment, is the key to success
7. Select a location with 180 degrees of visibility for your shooting position
8. Camouflage **does not hide movement**, Avoid all unnecessary movements
9. Never shoot at a sound or movement you cannot identify by body of the bird
10. Assume that all other sounds are being made by other hunters.

FINALLY

Don't hunt alone, take someone, especially try to take a kid, it is more fun. Remember that a mentor taught **you how** to hunt. Pass on your skills to the next person. Enjoy your turkey hunt, they are a superb resource, and are a lot of fun.

BIBLIOGRAPHY

AMO (Archery Trade Association Formerly AMO), Archery Trade Association, P.O. Box 70 New Ulm, MN 56073

Bulger, Jim. Colorado Parks and Wildlife. Turkey Hunting 101 - Turkey School/Chapter1. *About Turkey Hunting* by Jim Bulger, Hunter Outreach Program Coordinator, 2013

Clancy, Gary. *The Wild Turkey, Expert Advice for Locating and Calling Big Gobblers,* Creative Publishing, International, 5900 Green Oak Drive, Minnetonka, Minnesota 55343

Colorado Parks and Wildlife. *2012 Colorado Turkey*. Denver, Colorado, Hunting Application Brochure, and regulations 2012

Colorado Parks and Wildlife. *2013 Colorado Turkey*. Denver, Colorado, Hunting Application Brochure, and regulations, 201

Dickson, James G. *The Wild Turkey: Biology & Management*. Washington D.C. : National Wild Turkey Federation and U.S. Forest Service, 1992

Geiger, J Michael *TURKEY HUNTING 101, NARROWS MALLARD CLUB, INC.,* Lakewood, Colorado, 2013

IBO (International Bowhunting Organization) P.O. Box 398, Vermillion, OH 44089

Leopold, Aldo. *Game Management*. The University of Wisconsin Press, 1986, The University of Wisconsin System, 1930 Monroe St., Madison, Wisconsin 53711

Oliver, W. W., and R. A. Ryker. 1990. *Pinus ponderosa.* Pages 413-424 in R. M. Bums and B. H.Honkala, technical Coordinators. Silvics ofNorth America. United States Department ofAgriculture Forest Service Agriculture

Stratman, Marty R*., Ecology and Management of Rio Grande Turkeys in the South Platte River Corridor,* Technical Publication Number 45, May 2013, Colorado Parks and Wildlife

The National Wild Turkey Federation, Website http://www.nwtf.org/, Publication, *Turkey Country,* Headquarters, The Wild Turkey Center, 770 Augusta Road, Edgefield SC 29842

The Wildlife Techniques Manual, Management, Volume 2, 7th Edition, The Johns Hopkins University Press, Edited by Nova J. Silvy, 2012

Yarrow, Greg. Clemson University, Cooperative Extension, *Fact sheet 35: Biology and Mangement of Eastern Wild Turkey*. Revised 2009. Clemson, South Carolina, 2013

Picture – Michael Geiger

ABOUT THE AUTHOR

Picture – Michael Geiger

J. Michael Geiger developed his love for waterfowl and wildlife management when he first learned to hunt ducks along the S. Platte River near Orchard, Colorado with his father, as a youth of eleven years old.

He attended the University of Montana in Missoula, MT., majoring in Wildlife Management and Biology. He was in the USAF in Spain during the Vietnam era, before returning to the U of M. He then pursued his 25 year career in the family Real Estate business, followed by more than a decade in securities and financial management, while also pursuing a 20 year aquatic weed management career.

Completing college with a degree in Business Management and Marketing at University of Colorado, Denver, he never lost his fascination with the concept of actively attempting to put back more into the ecosystem than he and other hunters took out.

Never far from his passion, Michael purchased, with his father's help, the first 30 acres of river bottom along the S. Platte River in Morgan County Colorado, in the early 1970's. Over forty years later, his dream expanded to include many more acres of mixed river bottom, dry land grasses and "rehabilitation necessary" property.

His wife, Mary Ann has been a very active and a crucial part of this partnership since 1979. She is affectionately known as the "Duck Shack Mom" to all of the cold, hungry, and happy hunters using the property.

Today the property fledges more ducks, geese, and other game animals on the property than what has been harvested. Serious habitat improvement began in the early 1980's, with help from property hunters as the first of two dozen wood duck boxes were built and installed, followed shortly afterward by the development of ponds, several new quail shelters, and a couple dozen duck and goose nest structures. The creation of several food plots and the setting aside a fenced "No Man's Land" for the nesting of turkey and quail, as well as White Tail deer for fawning grounds, has been an added bonus. The property now hums with new young each spring.

Committed to sharing his experience in the practical application of habitat management on a small scale, he actively shares information about these successes with area game managers, landowners, hunting clubs, and service groups in Colorado and Wyoming.